Now,
My Perspective

Hannah Zuta

Suite 300 - 990 Fort St
Victoria, BC, V8V 3K2
Canada

www.friesenpress.com

Copyright © 2021 by Hannah Zuta
First Edition — 2021

Illustrations by Lorena Pantaleon Cabrera

All rights reserved.

No part of this publication may be reproduced in any form, or by any means, electronic or mechanical, including photocopying, recording, or any information browsing, storage, or retrieval system, without permission in writing from FriesenPress.

ISBN
978-1-5255-9437-3 (Hardcover)
978-1-5255-9436-6 (Paperback)
978-1-5255-9438-0 (eBook)

1. *Poetry, American*

Distributed to the trade by The Ingram Book Company

To be frank,

Being Black is an experience very few will be lucky enough to undergo. I do, however, think it's an experience that people should be able to understand.

Being Black is not a monolithic experience. It's a race; a label. My experience is not my neighbour's, nor is theirs mine.

Now, My Perspective

Desperation

Now, My Perspective

Pay Attention to What You Are, Pay Attention!

Take a look around at my town,
        Do you know your tone?
It's my own and I'm the only one allowed.
        You are not your own.
The skies are a sunny shade of orange.
        Do you know your tone?
The grass is a pretty shade of green.
        You are not your own!

I like to watch her and laugh;
the little town in which she finds solace
is it a figment, a dance, a trance?
The truth is waiting beyond the gates,
beyond the green grass and orange sky.

You're Black.
A Black girl
is all you are.
Please,

Take a look around my town.
Won't you please
Just take a look around,
I promise there's more.

Hannah Zuta

We're the Same, Don't Worry

Is it you?
Or you?
Is it them?
Or is it me?

Who's looking at the left strand
of my hair that's out of place?
Who's looking at the light spot
on the right side of my cheek?
Who's looking at the big lips
on my face?

Is it me?
Or you?
Who is it!

I promise it's no different than yours.
The bounce, the curl is the same
as yours.
Don't worry, I can make it the same.
Don't worry, it will be the same.

I have to make it the same.
I have to make it the same.
I have to make it the same.
I have to make it the same?

Now, My Perspective

I Get It Now!

You know I think I get it,
I finally understand.
If I just get like you,
I'll be fine.

When you say a word
         I'll repeat.
               Where you move
                    I'll follow.

When you go left
I'll be right behind you.
When you go down
         I'll
            fall
               with
                    you.

Clouded and confused,
she cried.
Clouded and confused
she cried tears that weren't even her own.

Pathetic.

Hannah Zuta

We Have No Name

When you look at me,
What do you see?
An opportunity?
Or an outlet?

Do you use me
to validate yourself?
Your behaviour?
What am I, your excuse?

It's ok I have a Black,
It's ok I have a Black,
It's ok I have a Black,
It's ok I have a Black.
Friend?

Please say I'm your friend.
Anything.
Just anything,
I'll take anything at this point.

Now, My Perspective

Let's Play A Little Game

A hint of hurt
A drop of annoyance
A sprinkle of longing
Mainly curiosity.

oh, to be you
just for a day
we could switch
I just want to see

what a world
that would be
no troubles or worries
oh, just to see

I could be you
You could be me
just for a day
just to see

You Have No Choice, Who Are You Without Them?

Grasping at masks,
trying on what fits,
discarding what doesn't.

there are too many to try
I'm drowning

Desperately pulling at the next
hoping for a different result.

It's maddening.
I have no choice.
I have to keep trying.

Now, My Perspective

We're All Black at the End of the Day

I like them medium,
I like them light,
I like them brown.
But don't get it twisted,
I will never like you.

"See, honey you're just too dark,"
says the guy.
"You don't really fit our mold,"
says the job.

It's nothing against you,
But don't get it twisted.
We'll never like you.

There's absolutely nothing you can do
but to sit there in your lonely blues.
Just sit there and remember,
always remember,
they'll never like you.

You say we're all Black
and that may be true.
But only one of us is getting beaten
for being a darker hue.

Colorism

Hannah Zuta

Colorism,
Colorism,
Colorism,

    I hate you.

Now, My Perspective

I Fundamentally Just Don't Understand

Why are we considered bottom of the barrel?
The last pick?
Every morning when I look in the mirror,
It's a constant reminder of a never-ending pit.

The birds that fly in the sky,
The screech of a bike stopping,
The sound of rain painting the ground,

These are all things I can understand.

The sly looks,
Unnerving conversation,
Masking me to appease you,

These things I just don't understand.

You know I meant to write about confusion,
A cornucopia of mixed sentiment
Constantly echoing and cocooning the clanging
Frustration and pure resentment conceived
Through cracked promises and cracked confidence

That has been tried and exhausted and crucified and
In case I haven't made it abundantly clear!

I fundamentally just don't understand.

Indignation

Now, My Perspective

For Kalu

Don't you dare tell me what to do!
Don't you dare tell me how to look!
You're lucky I give you the time of day,
You're lucky I even look your way.

If I don't want to wear socks in my shoes
Then my bare skin is what you'll see.
If I want kinks in my hair
Then that's exactly what it'll be.

I'm my own being,
You don't get to control me!

Focus on the mess you're in over there,
Stop projecting it onto me.

Hannah Zuta

They Want to Erase Me

I see myself in none of these.
Not a single one.
Not one lesson or story.
They want to erase me.

I stand and integrate,
I bend and assimilate,
I fall and homogenize,
agreeing to erase me.

They find joy in watching
knowing there's nothing I can do
to pick up the pen.
They want to erase me.

40

The past is as flawed as the present.
Stories twisted to suit a narrative,
epic tales of kings and chiefs
reduced to fables.

I have a problem with who has the pen.
They white out their sins and
transgressions,
they call me crazy
for making out the smudged ink.

For years I was blind
but now I can see.
People who had the pen,
still control people like me.

Oluwatoyin

Oluwatoyin is you,
Oluwatoyin is me.
She was pretty and vocal,
she was elegant and direct.

As gorgeous as the light glistening on
a beach wave
as youthful as the child playing outside.
Killed by the very same ones
she swore to protect.

Oluwatoyin could have been you.
Oluwatoyin could have been me.
We failed her every single step of
the way.
No one paid attention.

We will scream your name
from the top of the hill
that you sacrificed yourself on.

I see myself in her.
We all should.
In the whistling trees and the
blue skies,
I remember that you should still
be here.

Now, My Perspective

Oluwatoyin,
Forever nineteen.

These Men Ain't…

I bend and distort
to fit into your optics.
You sit there and criticize
straight as a board.

Help me!
Help me!
Educate me!
Treat me like a child!

I whisper
You talk
I talk
You yell

I promise.
Nothing will happen
if you just sit down
and listen.

Now, My Perspective

Watch, Don't Stare

I see you walking,
staring,
taking notes,
mimicking.

When you go and replicate
When you go show your friends
Let them know where you took it from

Let them know it's not organic.
Your vernacular, your hair, your style?
We had it.

Let them know what you stole.

Never giving credit where credit is due,
don't you know where all this started?
So, when you see your lil' friends,
let them know.

Hannah Zuta

Can't Keep Runnin' Away

Run run run
Constantly running
Run run run
From what you think is coming.

You better pray that he lets you
Pause, breathe, selah,
Pause, breathe, selah?
I'll just keep run run running.

Devil's in the water but
Hush!
Don't you dare speak his name.

Say amen amen.
You're torn in limbo?
Amen amen.
You're caught in constant turmoil?
Amen amen.

Why do we assume we're free?
For able is she that bears the burden.

Don't wait for me, selah.
Don't wait for me.

Now, My Perspective

I Despise You

I hate it here!
Why do I sit here?
Grasping at straws,
for those who'll never understand.

Appeasing people
who deep down
will never know
what's it's like to be me!

What have I been reduced to?

I erase my tongue,
erase my hair,
my colour,
Me.

I do it for you,
all for you,
everything is for you!
Meanwhile, who are you?

Hannah Zuta

Well If This Is It, I Might as Well Get Comfortable

If this is permanent
then what's the point?
If things will never change,
then I'll just go about the rest of my days

not really caring
not really trying
it's been going on so long
what would a person like me change?

I'll remain mute.
Apathy and complacency.
What a sickening combination.

I've walked this ground, yes, I've walked this ground.

I'll end up like most,
Just sinking,
            sinking,
                sinking,
Waiting for the shadowman to come.

Have we hit the heavens?

Now, My Perspective

Are You the Problem?

God it's hard looking at you!
What is wrong with you?
Why can't you just be yourself?
Just be you!

But you too,
who are you?
Me, you,
honestly, I haven't a clue.

I hope when I find you
it'll be true.
Hopefully when I find you
I'll love you for you.

Reflections and Introspection

Now, My Perspective

How About We Wait Just
A Little Bit Longer

Trapped in a cage of flesh,
feet wrapped in chains
somehow still curious
as to what the day might bring.

Walking and rattling
slowly trudging along
as People watch in shock.

Deem it a curse,
the curiosity to see
what the next day might bring.

In spite of animosity and hanging trees
I still have the desire to see
what the next day might bring.

Hannah Zuta

Will You Forget About Me?

When I leave
please don't forget about me.

I know eventually you'll go
I know eventually I will too,
but please don't forget about me.

I hope I'm not an idea
doomed to be rehearsed
and never played.
Do the tears of my brothers rain over me?
Do the tears of my sisters rain over me?

What will linger—
my self-criticisms?
or conversations?

I don't know how long I'll stay.
Everything is taken for granted
'til you realize you're anything
and nothing at all.

I know everyone goes someday,
I know we're all fragile and made of clay,
But I hope you won't forget about me.

Now, My Perspective

I Often Wonder

How do others see me?
Am I a blip in your day?
Or do I linger a little longer?

I'll never know how you see me.
Should I make an effort to stand out?
Or should I be content,
blending into your thoughts.

Well, what are thoughts
if not blips of things that stand out,
momentary   short-circuits   that   ebb
and flow.

I often wonder,
What do you notice first?
Skin, teeth, hair?
I often wonder,
why exactly do I care?

After all
we're all just blips
in each other's minds.

We ebb and flow.
Like the river.

Hannah Zuta

Seasons Come and Seasons Go

Everything goes eventually.
The tide changes eventually.
You'll see me eventually.
Eventually I'll be here waiting.

Until then let's take a seat.
Listen to me and I'll do the same.
Tell me your problems and I'll tell you mine.

Hopefully we each find our own solace.
My problem isn't my own.
It's your perception—
but that ebbs and flows.

While we wait for the tide,
I slowly realize
it's all up to me and my eyes.

Now, My Perspective

A Replacement

To find your place
what a wonderful fleeting feeling.
I hope I find mine.

Being cradled by you and only you.
No external person needed,
I hope you find yours.

A place to grow and learn
with no fear of judgement or malice.
I hope I find mine.

Well, when I do I'll say,

Farewell I,
hope you fare well
Farewell I,
hope you fare well

Farewell I,
           hope you fare well.

Nights

Biking through these nights
no one can bother me
when I'm biking
        biking
           biking
through these nights.

Walking through these nights,
no one can bother me
when I'm walking
        walking
           walking
through these nights.

The night and I have an agreement.
It doesn't bother me,
I don't bother it.

When the day comes
I sink back into my music,
sinking
        sinking
           sinking
just waiting for the night.

Don't wait for me sunshine,
don't wait for me.

Now, My Perspective

Nightingale

I heard the nightingales
singing my prophecy
since before I was born.

Telling me what will happen,
what should happen,
when it would happen.

Bless the nightingales
for their cries of warning.
May you find your own solace.

They guided me through,
abandoning their own haven
to help me find mine.

Bless the nightingale.
I have the night,
I hope you find yours.

May solace keep you well.

Oh the Colours, Oh the Shades

I look around
and what do I see?
All the colours
surrounding me.

They change
the farther you go along.
The more to see
the more to admire.

No longer a blip,
but a ray of confidence shining through me.
Oh, how fun it is to finally see
all the shades and colours surrounding me.

Now, My Perspective

Friends

The first and the last
vital no matter the say.
You are the reason I am who I am.

To the ones who watch from above
who were robbed of another day,
you are a part of who I am.

A tie as strong roots
and as deep as the river that feeds it
In pieces and distant cracks
a part of me and a part of you.

Thank you for making me who I am,
forever with you.

Hannah Zuta

Made In His Image

From the night to the day
From the sun to the moon
From me to you,
I'd like to thank Awurade for the day.

Now, My Perspective

For Maya! For Nina!

It ain't all too bad,
I have my country
and I have my flag.

You can stand there and watch me parade
knowing you will never know
the ins and outs of my people's game.

Sit there in ignorance
or wallow in shame.
It's all the same to me.

Cry, beg, weep,
just know that I'll be here
calmly counting sheep.

See, because finally
you might know what it's like to be me.

Sinnerman
Sinnerman
Sinnerman
Sinnerman

Oh sinnerman!
Don't you know the rock can't hide you?

Nuerteki

Cheers,
raise a glass!
For the ones who have their lens on me,
for the ones who never got the chance.

I'm Black, I'm proud.
From the Adangbe village where the chief eats
to the Fante coast shores where the slaves left,
everywhere I go it follows me around.

Across this Atlantic
I'll never know peace
with these judging eyes.

When did the king's crown
cease to hold any weight?
When did the words from my tongue
cease to hold any weight?

Awurade, meda wo ase,
for Jehovah is worthy of all praise!
Awurade,
Awurade meda wo ase,
for Jehovah is worthy of all praise!

Now, My Perspective

Pause
Take a moment
Selah

Nuerteki,
the granddaughter my father's parents
never got to see.
Nuerteki,
the granddaughter my mother's parents
never got to see.
I hope I've done y'all proud.
For the ones who have their lens on me,
I hope I've done y'all proud.

Awurade meda wo ase,
Nuerteki.

CPSIA information can be obtained
at www.ICGtesting.com
Printed in the USA
LVHW071531010421
683005LV00031B/149/J